LOVED
NO MATTER WHAT!

Written by Shealyn Visser
Illustrated by Naomi Edwards

Loved No Matter What is based on the works of
Dr. Tim Kimmel, with permission. To learn more about
the Grace Based Blueprint, visit gracebased.com.

Published by Gracebased Publishing
© Shealyn Visser, 2025
All rights reserved
ISBN: 979-8-9989594-0-0

Learn more at gracebased.com

For my sons, Jackson & Kyden.
May you always know how loved you are.
- Shealyn

For my family, thank you for
being my most cherished supporters.
- Naomi

I am LOVED NO MATTER WHAT!
That means I can...

Be my CRAZY, ZANY self!

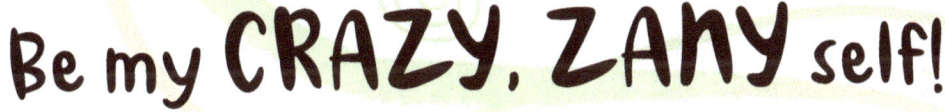

Dream GREAT BIG amazing dreams!

Never ever,
EVER
give up!

Do things my own FUNKY MONKEY way!

Be up and down and **UPSIDE DOWN!**

Talk and talk and TALK about what I think and feel.

Face WHATEVER comes my way.

Choose what's **RIGHT**,
even when it's hard.

Make a **GOOD** day out of a bad one.

Be BRAVE, even when I'm scared.

Let someone else be the **STAR**.

Say **THANK YOU** for everything, every day and in every way.

Make a **BIG** difference,
no matter how young I am!

CONNECT AS A FAMILY!

1. Take time as a family to share what makes each person special.

2. Enjoy a messy family activity like baking or a puzzle. Have the child notice the big mess as you go. Point out how you made something beautiful (or delicious) together.

Find Gracebased parenting books, videos, and more resources at gracebased.com